Hidden Objects You'll (Almost) Never Find

Illustrated by Don Channen

Introduction by Eva Weiss

ST. HELIER, JERSEY

Cover design: Benjie Herskowitz

ISBN: 0-943706-15-7

Printed in Hungary

It's true, some of the **UH! OH!** characters inside this book are pretty easy to find.

But watch out! Only 7 out of 10 kids tested between the ages of 8-12 were able to find all the **UH! OH!** Hanukkah characters, and the four hidden objects in each picture, within one hour.

If you can find the **UH! OH!** characters and the four hidden objects in each picture within one hour, just fill out the form on the last page of this book and we'll make you an official **UH! OH!** TESTER.

You'll receive a sneak preview of our next **UH! OH!** title and get a chance to test your skills against our **UH! OH!** artists and writers.

INTRODUCTION

In this book, every illustration tells a story. Take a careful look at each picture and find the character in trouble -- the one who says the words **UH! OH!**

Then find the Menorah in the corner of each illustration. Inside the Menorah, there are four more objects for you to find. They are all hidden somewhere in the picture.

Of course each picture tells you about the holiday of Hanukkah. You remember why we celebrate Hanukkah, don't you?

Did you say **UH! OH!***? Well, here are some clues to help you refresh your memory. Read them, then look at the illustrations inside.*

TANKS BUT NO TANKS

Why would soldiers dare to fight huge elephants? Those soldiers were Maccabees, the leaders of the Jewish people, and they fought against the legions of the ancient Greek Empire. At that time, over two thousand years ago, the Jews were the only people in the world who believed in one God. Even though the Jews were much fewer in number, they went to war because it was the only way that they could continue their belief. They fought bravely and won -- even against the legions of elephants.

CHECK THE OIL, PLEASE!

After their victory, the Jewish people returned to their Temple in Jerusalem. They wanted to relight the Menorah, a symbol of peace. As you'll see, the oil checkers searched hard to find the special pure oil needed to light the Menorah. One small jar of pure oil was found, and miraculously, it lasted for eight days.

TEMPLE DEDICATION

The light from the Menorah brought joy to the Temple Dedication. The Levites returned to their musical instruments without missing a beat. It was no secret that everyone enjoyed the festivities, even the undercover agents at table 007.

CANDLE TOWN

To celebrate Hanukkah today, we light a nine-branched Menorah. Eight candles are lit for the eight days of Hanukkah. The ninth candle, called the Shamash, lights the others. The Hanukkah Menorah is lit as soon as night falls. Can you find all the candle people in candle town rushing to make it home before dark?

LATKA PALACE

Who are those potato heads from another planet? They've landed at Latka Palace because they want to eat oil-fried potato pancakes. Why? Because it reminds them of the miracle of the oil -- and because they like the taste.

PAC DREIDLE

Why chase after a runaway dreidle? Because it's a great way to enjoy Hanukkah. Most dreidles have Hebrew letters that form the sentence, "A Great Miracle Happened There." Dreidles from Israel, however, say, "A Great Miracle Happened Here." Here or there, the dreidles in this picture seem to have a mind of their own.

*Inside this book, you'll find many more illustrated pictures that have to do with the story and customs of Hanukkah. They'll start you thinking. But don't get too lost in thought because -- **UH! OH!** -- you only have 1 hour to find the **UH! OH!** Hanukkah characters, and the four hidden objects in each picture.*

Good luck!

TANKS, BUT NO TANKS!

Before tanks--there were elephants. The Maccabees had to use special tactics to conquer these giant grey Greek behemoths. Getting some squeaky mice to scare the elephants helped, but Judah and his men had some other secret weapons too. Can you find them?

——Find——

Bucket

UH! OH!

Axe

Flower Pot

Peanut

CHECK THE OIL, PLEASE!

The Greeks used all the Temple oil for idol worship. There was no pure oil left. But then the oil checkers found a small jar of oil. It lasted for 8 days. Question: Who put all those olives in that little bitty jar?

——Find——

Section of Pipe

Lunchbox

Bowling Ball

Chess Rook

TEMPLE DEDICATION

After many battles, the Jews re-captured their Temple. The Levites once again struck-up the band, and sang the psalms. Thousands came to celebrate, and they all found room...even without reserved seating.

——Find——

Upside Down Meatball

Table Sign

Musical Note

Elephant

RIGHT, WRONG, LEFT, RIGHT

On Hanukkah it pays to know your right from left. Remember, you put the candles in from right to left, but light them from left to right. If you're watching someone light candles his left is your right, and your right is his left, although your left is always your left...right?

——— Find ———

Bow tie

Cap

Net

Coffe Pot

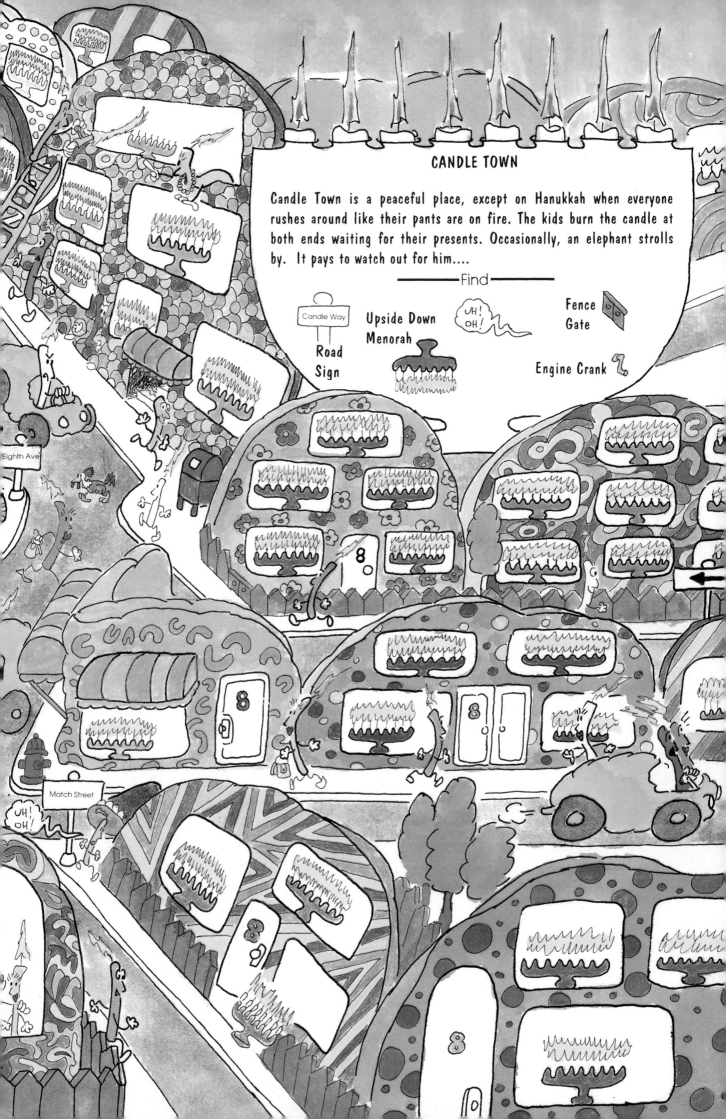

CANDLE TOWN

Candle Town is a peaceful place, except on Hanukkah when everyone rushes around like their pants are on fire. The kids burn the candle at both ends waiting for their presents. Occasionally, an elephant strolls by. It pays to watch out for him....

———— Find ————

Candle Way

Road Sign

UH! OH!

Upside Down Menorah

UH! OH!

Fence Gate

Engine Crank

MY, WHAT BIG TEETH YOU HAVE...

Jeremy is off to grandmother's house. She's anxiously waiting for him to bring the jar of olive oil so she can light her Hanukkah menorah. But Jeremy has to be careful to follow the dreidle signs to grandmother's house. UH! OH! Can you help him avoid the obstacles in his path?

——Find——

Match Stick

Sea Monster Tail

Periscope

Green Menorah

RUN, LATKA, RUN!

Do too many chefs scare the food? Some of these dishes just don't want to be served. See those potato pancakes trying to escape? But don't worry, the ingredients for more latkas are around somewhere. Can you find them?

————— Find —————

Flour

Egg

Salt Shaker

Oil

Potato

LAS OY VEYGAS

Holidays are not the time to gamble. But in a dreidle casino you use only funny money. Want to play? Twirl the dreidle. Watch it land. If it's a Nun--you lose! Gimel--you win! Shin--skip your turn! Hey--split the pot! Now, try your luck.

——Find——

Turtle

UH! OH!

Slot machine
Window

Cent Sign

Webbed Foot

PAC DREIDLE

Hanukkah dreidles love to twirl their tops. But after a long, hard day of being chased by a hungry pac dreidle, it's good to know there's a dreidle doctor on call. That way they can limp on in, get fixed up, and head out again for a spin!

———— Find ————

Hammer

Dreidle with Glasses

Stopwatch

UH! OH!

Four leaf Clover

THE GOLEM DREIDLE

Before Superman, there was the Golem; a mud-made superhero ready to help the Jewish people whenever they are in trouble. He comes in all shapes and sizes. But don't try making one yourself. You have to know just the right words to create him, wake him... and control him.

——— Find ———

Hamburger
Hat

UH!
OH!

Two-headed
Spear

Roller
Skates

Mudpie

How Well Did You Do?

TIME

Me   _____

Mom   _____

Dad   _____

Brother   _____

Sister   _____

Friend   _____

If you found all of the **UH! OH!** characters and the four hidden objects in each picture within 1 hour, then you qualify as an **UH! OH!** TESTER. Send in your Name, Address (city, state, zip) and Time to:

UH! OH! TESTER
POB 101
Woodmere, New York 11598

You'll receive a sneak preview of our next **UH! OH!** title and get a chance to test your skills against our **UH! OH!** artists and writers.